Common La
Trainin

CONTENTS

1. Introduction --- 5
2. Two Great Principles of Natural Law -------------------- 7
3. Natural Liberty and the Basis of Common Law
       Courts: First Principles - [1-10] ---------------------- 8
4. How do we use Common Law? --------------------------- 11
5. Matters before a Common Law Court ----------------- 12
6. Establishing and Maintaining Common Law Courts - 15
7. Legal Procedure and Control Protocol ------------------ 18
8. Step One - Compiling the Case ----------------------------19
9. Step Two - Seeking the Remedy of a Common Law
       Court - Filing a Notice of Claim of Right ----------20
10. Step Three - Forming a Common Law Court --------20
11. Step Four - Swearing in and Convening the Jury
       and Court Officers: Oaths of Office ----------------21
12. Step Five - Pre-trial Conference -------------------------21
13. Step Six - Issuing of Public Summonses -------------- 22
14. Step Seven - The Trial Commences: Opening
       Arguments --- 22
15. Step Eight - The Main Proceedings -------------------- 23
16. Step Nine - Closing Summaries and Arguments
       to the Jury and final advice by the Adjudicator --23
17. Step Ten - The Jury retires to deliberate ------------- 24
18. Step Eleven - The Jury issues its unanimous
       verdict and sentence ----------------------------------- 24

19. **Step Twelve - The Court adjourns and the Sentence is enforced** ---------------------------------- 24

20. **Verdicts, Enforcement and Convicting Rulers and Institutions** -- 26

21. **Enforcement** -- 27

22. **Common Law Sheriffs and Peace Officers** ----------- 32

23. **On Citizens' Arrests** -- 35

24. **The Procedure for performing a citizens' arrest** --- 35

25. **Broader Consequences of the Common Law Court: A World Made New** -------------------------- 36

26. **Appendix** -- 39

27. **A. Sources and Resourses** ------------------------------ 40

28. **B. Examples of Common Law Counrt Documents -** 41

29. **1. Notice of Claim of Right** ----------------------------- 41

30. **2. Deputizing Notice issued by Court Sheriff to other Peace Officers** ------------------------------- 42

31. **3. Documents in the first case of The International Common Law Court of Justice** ---- 44

32. **C. Strategy and Tactics: Forty Key Lessons from Sun Tsu** --- 44

33. **What is the International Tribunal into Crimes of Church and State?** ------------------------------------- 50

34. **What is the International Common Law Court of Justice?** -------------------------------------- 52

35. **Nominee for the Nobel Peace Prize (2013)** ----------- 54

2

JUSTICE, HONOR, MERCY

The Purpose of a Common Law court

Many people are plagued by the injustice of the courts, police, schools, banks, social services and the NHS.

As citizens of a common law based judicial system, we have the right *to come together* in our local communities *and convene* a common law court in full lawful legitimacy.

We are capable of judging and sentencing any person, business or organization fairly regardless of the status they hold in society.

A court convened randomly by the public can be trusted to judge fairly with no alterior motives.

Our sentences are enforced by local community members acting as peace officers who are sworn agents of the court directed by our court appointed sheriff.

Common Law Community Training Manual

Establishing the Reign of Natural Liberty:
The Common Law and its Courts

A Community Training Manual

Issued by The International Tribunal into Crimes of Church and State (Brussels)

What is assembling is the first court in history to bring judgment against the Vatican and the Crown of England as institutions. But our Court also signals **the dawn of a new notion of justice: one defined by the people themselves,** and especially by the historic victims of church and state, to bring about not only a judgment on their persecutors, but a new political and spiritual arrangement to undo the systems responsible for **inter-generational crimes against humanity**

— from the founding Charter of The International Common Law Court of Justice, September 1, 2012.

Introduction

History was made on February 11, 2013, when the first Catholic Pope in history resigned from his office during peacetime in order to avoid arrest for protecting and aiding child raping priests.

Barely two weeks later, the same Pope Benedict, Joseph Ratzinger, was found guilty by the **International Common Law Court of Justice** for Crimes against Humanity, including child trafficking. And the Arrest Warrant that he had anticipated, and which provoked his resignation, was issued against him on February 25.

Evading justice inside the Vatican, Ratzinger is presently an **international fugitive** from the law – and a living example of the power of Common Law courts to successfully prosecute so-called "heads of state".

The lawful verdict of the **International Common Law Court of Justice** was a "shot heard around the world" that has spawned efforts in twenty one countries to establish similar **popular courts of justice** to reclaim the law from the wealthy and their compliant governments. (see www.itccs.org)

This Manual provides instruction and training to those of you who have moved from words to actions. We speak to those who not only recognize **the permanent war being waged against humanity by a global corporate tyranny,** but who are actively engaged in dismantling **that murderous system** at its source so that justice can be made real in a reclaimed world.

You are part of a growing movement to create a new, liberated society within the shell of the old by first allowing the law to act for all people and not a clique of judicial specialists and their friends. That new society is emerging through every act of courage and integrity by we who know what is at stake, and that is, our children and the future of our species.

Why we are Taking Action: Freeing Ourselves by Remembering the True Law:

"Man is born free; yet everywhere he is in chains."

That fact has **altered little** over the centuries. But the chains of oppression over much of our species have been forged through the weapons of violence and ignorance, and they can be undone.

Long before any rulers held sway over humanity, **men and women established customs and laws among themselves to ensure their peace and liberties as free, self-governing people.** They did so from an inherent recognition of a Natural

Law of Equality or Divine Law whereby no one has any right to dominate or rule over others, to seize more of creation than another, or to own any part of a world given equally to all people.

It is the Divine Principle of Creation that **every child born is endowed with unalienable liberties that no authority, law, government or religion can diminish or abolish.** Any power that attempts to do so is tyrannical and illegitimate, even if it operates according to its own laws – for such tyranny is a denial of the natural order and an attack upon divinity and humanity.

Two great principles summarize this Natural Law:

1. All things exist and are held in common. By the state of nature, no one has any more of a claim to the earth than another, as noted by a founder of modern law, Thomas Hobbes:

"I demonstrate in the first place, that in the natural state of men (which state we may properly call the state of nature) all men have equal right unto all things" (Leviathan, 1651)

2. The Law does harm to no-one. (*Actus Regis Nemini Facit Injuriam*) Arising from the Ten Commandments and God's law to do no harm to one's neighbor, this principle forms the basis of modern law.

John Stuart Mill articulated this principle in *On Liberty* where he argued that, "The only purpose for which power can be rightfully exercised over any member of a civilized community, against his will, is to prevent harm to others." (1869)

An equivalent idea was earlier stated in France's *Declaration of the Rights of Man and of the Citizen* of 1789 as, **"Liberty consists in the freedom to do everything which injures no one else;** hence the exercise of the natural rights of each man has no limits except those which assure to the other members of the society the enjoyment of the same rights. These limits can only be determined by law."

This Natural Law exists to maintain the natural peace and equity between people and is their shield and protector against unjust rule, rather than a force over them. Within the ancient traditions of tribal communities, especially in the Anglo-Saxon world, this Law evolved into what became known as the **Customary** or **Common Law**, or **the Law of the Land**. It has strong echoes in the customs of indigenous nations all over the world.

Here is a basic summary of the nature of True or Common Law versus arbitrary law.

Natural Liberty and the Basis of Common Law Courts: First Principles

1. Every man, woman and child is born and is by nature free, equal and sovereign, and possesses an inherent knowledge of what is true and right. Accordingly, no-one can be subordinated to another or to any external authority, since every person's inherent wisdom and liberty makes them complete and sufficient creations in themselves, within a wider community of equals.

2. This personal sovereignty is a reflection of the wider Natural Law, whereby all life by nature is indivisible and placed in common for the survival and happiness of all. In any just society, this commonality endows all people with the unalienable right to establish among themselves their own governance, and defend themselves against any tyranny or violence, including that inflicted by external authorities. Any authority that rules unjustly and arbitrarily, without the free and uncoerced consent of the people, has lost its right to rule and can be lawfully overthrown. "Unjust government is not government but tyranny" – Plato

3. This Natural Law gives rise to customary Common Law whose purpose is to protect the inherent liberties and sovereignty of men and women in a community by maintain-

ing equity and peace among them. The Common Law derives its authority from the people themselves, and from the capacity of the people to know what is just and to judge right and wrong for themselves. This capacity is expressed in a jury system of twelve freely chosen people who are the ultimate judge and authority under Common Law and its courts.

4. Historically, Common Law arose in England after the 11th century Norman Conquest as a bulwark in defense of the people against the arbitrary rule of self-appointed elites, especially monarchs and popes. The authority of these elites was derived unnaturally, from warfare, violent conquest and the theft of the earth, rather than from the consent of the community and its basis, the divine law of peace and equality. This elite rule arose most strongly in the Roman Empire and its descendent, the Church of Rome, under whose beliefs "god" is a dominator and conqueror ("domine"), and all people are "subjects" of the Pope.

5. Such a conquest-based rule of papal and kingly elites gave rise to a legal system known as Civil or Roman Law, and the belief that men and women are not endowed with the capacity for self-rule and wisdom. All law and authority is therefore derived externally, from statutes devised and imposed by a ruler, whether a pope, a monarch or a government. This system developed from Aristotelian philosophy and Roman property law in which creation is divided and human beings are treated as chattels and the possessions of others, and are thereby devoid of inherent liberties. The people are thus in every sense enslaved, cut off from the world given freely and in common to all. This slave system ranks and categorizes all people, and grants restricted "freedoms" (freithoms, or slave privileges) that are defined and limited through statutes issued by rulers.

6. Common and Civil (Roman) Law are therefore fundamentally opposed and are at war with each other. They cannot be reconciled, since they arise from two completely different notions of humanity and justice: Common Law knows life as a free gift given equally to all, while under Civil Law, life is a conditional privilege, and humanity is a managed slave populace. Accordingly, governments operate in practice according to Civil (statute) law and denigrate or ignore Common Law altogether through the rule of unaccountable judge-dominated courts.

7. The most extreme form of elite-based Civil/Roman Law is what is called Papal or Canon Law, which defines the Church of Rome as the only legitimate authority on earth to which all other laws, people and governments are subordinate. Canon law is self-governing and completely unaccountable to anything but itself. Behind its front of Christian rhetoric, Roman Catholicism is a neo-pagan cult based upon the late 3rd century Roman Emperor-worship system known as Sol Invictus, in which one sovereign entitled "God and Master" (Deus et Dominus) rules heaven and earth: specifically, the Pope. This tyrannical cult has not surprisingly caused more warfare, genocide, conquest and murder than any power in human history, and continues to constitute the single greatest threat to Common Law and human liberty.

8. The Church of Rome was the first and is the oldest corporation on our planet: a legal entity designed for the protection of tyrants, which nullifies the individual liability and responsibility of the elites for any crime or conquest they perpetrate. From Rome and the Incorporated Vatican has spread the contagion that now threatens to destroy our planet and our lives, as the unaccountable corporate oligarchy everywhere subverts liberty and the health of our planet by subordinating all of life to profit and power.

9. At this very moment of corporate conquest and its subjugation of humanity, a counter-movement is arising to reassert the divine purpose and its operation through the Common Law, and to restore the earth and humanity to their

natural being as a common body. This movement is foretold Biblically and in prophecy as the time when all the people are returned to their natural equality, devoid of all divisions, privileges and oppression, in order live in harmony with creation and one another.

10. This restoration of humanity is a divine purpose, and begins by actively dis-establishing all existing authority and institutions derived from Roman civil law, and replacing them with a new governance under Common Law jurisdiction. The creation of that new Natural Law authority among a liberated humanity is the fundamental purpose of the Common Law Courts.

How Do We Use the Common Law?

The truth is that throughout everyday life, people everywhere use and rely on Common Law to live and work together. It is simply the inherent way that people conduct their affairs together. Liken it to the roots that bind together human communities by unconditionally upholding the life, dignity and well-being of every man, woman and child. These roots are especially necessary and foundational in the face of tyrannical powers that seek to subvert such natural freedom.

The Common Law's firm horizontal guarantees of mutual respect and protection are a permanent threat to the efforts by arbitrary rulers to harness men and women into the unnatural and vertical arrangement known as the State. This is why every government and religion seeks to annul the Common Law with their own authority and statutes, in order to reduce free peoples everywhere to the status of regimented, obedient tax paying wage slaves who serve a ruling clique.

To extend our everyday reign of Common Law into all areas of life means to challenge the arbitrary rule of those cliques, and of all State level regimes. But the very fact that it is the Law of we, the vast majority of humanity, means that it only needs to be consistently practiced by enough of us for arbitrary authority and dangers to crumble.

We use the Common Law by simply employing and relying on it, in all spheres of life. And that means, **by first establishing functioning Common Law Courts with absolute and ultimate jurisdiction over every aspect of our communities and lives.**

Matters before a Common Law Court

Traditionally, law in the European tradition falls into **two general categories: civil and criminal law.** The former deals with disputes between individuals – often called "Tort" offenses – or issues of negligence which cause harm. Criminal law deals with acts of intentional harm to individuals but which, in a larger sense, are offences against all people because they somehow threaten the community.

Arising as a defense against absolutism and state or church tyranny, the Common Law traditionally has dealt with Criminal Law matters that "crown" or "canon law" courts refuse either to address, or do so in a restricted manner, including murder, rape, warfare and other crimes against the community. But civil matters of personal disputes may also be brought into a Common Law Court, which after all claims universal jurisdiction over all legal matters within a community.

Indeed, because Common Law is rooted in the jury system, what better forum can there be for the settling of civil matters between individuals than a trial before one's own neighbors?

For our purposes, however, the major focus of litigation before our Common Law Courts will be on Criminal Law and matters involving serious threats or crimes made against people, animals, communities, and the environment.

As in any lawful system, the burden of proof in any such litigation brought before the Common Law Court will be on the plaintiffs – those bringing the lawsuit – and normal Rules of Evidence will apply. For example, allegations against a party cannot be made in court without there being a basis in provable facts, such as primary documentation that is certified by an independent party, or by producing eyewitnesses to the alleged crime.

Another crucial Rule of Evidence is the inadmissibility of hearsay evidence, as in "No, I wasn't there, but I heard about what happened". This is an especially relevant rule when it comes to the commission of serious crimes, such as murder, genocide or rape.

In short, any allegation must be backed up with provable facts, and must be made by one who was a direct participant in or an eyewitness to the event.

For our purposes, it must be noted that in the case of especially monstrous, corporate crimes committed by governments or other powers, such as wars of aggression, genocide or human trafficking, normal rules of evidence are less stringently applied. This is because of a realistic understanding that **crimes committed by entire societies or regimes are of a different nature than crimes by isolated individuals.** A different set of norms regarding intent and provable evidence applies.

In the words of the chief American prosecutor at the Nuremberg Trials in 1946, Robert Jackson,

"No regime that seeks the extermination of entire groups of people generally retains written proof of their intent to commit this crime. Considering the murderous nature of their regime, there is no need, since such extermination is not considered a crime. Nevertheless, even such a system seeks to fog and dissimulate the evidence, especially during wartime … The proof of crimes against humanity generally lies not in documents but in the witness of survivors, remains in mass graves, and in the implied proof of the intent to commit these crimes contained in the everyday and institutionalized laws, attitudes and norms of the murderous regime." (our emphasis)

Implied intent is a legal concept especially relevant and specific to litigation involving genocidal regimes, including governments and churches whose world view and laws consider other groups to be unworthy of life or equal rights, such as the groups that were tried and sentenced in the first case of the International Common Law Court of Justice concerning the genocide of indigenous peoples in Canada by church and state. (www.itccs.org)

Laws such as the Indian Act of Canada, which impose a different set of laws on a racially targeted group, or the Roman Catholic "canon law" called Crimen Solicitations, which condones and facilitates the concealment of child rape within the church, indicate a clear implied intent to commit and abet criminal acts.

That is, it is unnecessary to prove the individual intent to harm children by Catholic priests, since under their own self-governing rules called "canon law", **every priest is systematically required to harm children by aiding those who do so if he is to retain his ordination and job.** The collective guilt of these clergy as a whole is implied and clear, just as it was concerning all of the servants of the Nazi regime.

Thus, while normal due process requires that the prosecution prove that the accused committed an act and did so with deliberate intent, such an intent may also be assumed to exist by the larger context of a crime, especially when that crime is perpetrated by entire organizations or regimes.

Ascertaining the truth is always laborious, but **ultimately the process is best guaranteed by a body of jurors than single adjudicators.** Common law juries, and not individual judges, are invariably a better guarantee against the abuse of Rules of Evidence and just procedure in a courtroom.

Self-governing judges are notoriously prone to corruption and political manipulation, and when appointed by the very governments under criminal investigation, are obviously unsuited to the task of rendering a fair judgment. In fact, under legal procedure, such state-appointed judges have no jurisdictional competence to rule on the criminality and guilt of their employers.

Judges routinely waive just procedure and rules of evidence, and are authorized to do so by statute law. In Canada, "crown" appointed judges even have the power to alter or destroy court records, silence one party in a dispute, and ignore due process altogether!

The whole point of establishing a **jury-run Common Law Court** is to prevent such a manipulation of the law and justice by unaccountable parties or vested interests. It is not accidental that a Founding Father of the American Republic, John Hancock, declared in 1777,

"If we have not Courts that are established and maintained by the People, rather than by bribable Judges, then we will have no Republic … Our Constitution and our Nation will rise or fall according to the independence of our Courts."

Establishing and Maintaining Common Law Courts

The Common Law's First Principles establish its general legitimacy and lawfulness. This valid system gives rise to Courts with the power to protect the people as a whole by prosecuting and indicting any persons and institutions that threaten the community.

The mandate to establish such Courts is derived from the sovereignty of the people as a whole, and not from any particular political system or government. **Common Law Courts are**

15

therefore universal, not constricted by customary borders or laws, and are jurisdictionally competent to adjudicate any issue or grievance. Common Law Courts are not subject to and do not recognize any other legal or moral authority, immunity or privilege, like those routinely claimed by heads of churches and states.

Enjoying universal jurisdiction because of its rootedness in the Natural Law, **Common Law Courts can be established in any country or community,** and not only within nations with a specifically common law legal tradition, such as England, Canada and America.

Common Law Courts are established when any number of men and women come together to judge a matter of concern to them and to their community. Thus, such Courts are invariably and naturally linked to political movements, "town hall gatherings" and Tribunals of Conscience that unite citizens and give direct voice to their concerns and demands. The Court is thereby the expression of that voice.

The Court itself is established by the direct will and vote of the people as a whole, who elect a Citizen Jury of at least twelve people, a Citizen Prosecutor to conduct the case on behalf of the people, a presiding Adjudicator whose job is strictly advisory, and a Sheriff and group of Peace Officers to enforce the summonses, warrants and verdicts of the Court.

Additionally, the community may appoint **local magistrates** versed in the law known as **Justices of the Peace** (JP's), who traditionally have the power to summon juries and issue warrants. The JP may also initiate the formation of a Common Law court.

All of the participants in a Common Law Court **must present their own case** in all of the Court proceedings, since to allow another to "re-present" them would constitute a surrender of their **natural rights and sovereignty.** This applies both to the plaintiffs and the defendants involved in any matter before the Court.

There are, accordingly, no professional lawyers or permanent presiding judges in a Common Law Court system.

There is no restriction on the power of a Common Law Court to access any person, place or thing, nor any limitation on the duration or rights of the Court. The Court and its Magistrate can issue Public Summonses that are binding on any person or institution, and enforceable by the **Court Sheriff** who has an unrestricted right to detain any person named in the Summons and bring them into Court.

The final verdict of the **Common Law Court Jury** is final and not subject to appeal, simply because a reasonable and non-coerced group of citizens can come to the truth of any matter on the basis of the evidence alone, possessed as they are of an inherent knowledge of right and wrong. **The truth is not mutable.** A defendant is either innocent or guilty; the truth is not subject to revision or reconsideration, since it then is not true.

However, if it can be proven beyond any doubt that the Court's verdict was made unlawfully, was unduly influenced, or occurred on the basis of incomplete or faulty evidence, a Common Law Magistrate can re-open and re-try the case with the normal Jury and Court officers.

In the same way, the sentence of the Court is also final, and is enforced not only by the **Court Sheriff** but by all citizens. For the Common Law arises from and is the direct responsibility of all people, as are all of its procedures. The verdict really is a declaration of the people that they will govern themselves according to their own democratic law and decisions.

There is no restriction on the power of a Citizen Jury to impose a sentence on any person, group or institution. The Court Adjudicator or Magistrate has no power to alter, influence or direct the original verdict or sentence of the Jury – simply to advise the

Jury on legal procedure and points of law.

Finally, upon issuing its final verdict and sentence, the **Common Law Court Jury** is automatically concluded and its members are released from their duty. No Court is maintained without the conscious consent and participation of the people themselves.

Again, there is no professional, permanent caste of either lawyers or judges in a Common Law Court system, but rather elected and temporary Court officers.

Legal Procedure and Court Protocol

Common Law, being derived from Natural Justice, bases its legal procedures **on the centrality of Due Process:** the three-fold right of anyone to be notified of the charges being brought against him, to see the evidence in such a suit, and to be tried and judged before his own peers.

No legitimate trial can proceed nor can a conviction be rendered if the accused has not been given these rights, and afforded the chance to freely defend himself in a court of law.

Such rights are based on these fundamental doctrines of the Common Law:

1. It is presumed that the accused is innocent, not guilty;

2. The burden of proof of the accused's guilt rests not upon the defendant but the plaintiff, who must convince a jury of the guilt of the accused beyond any reasonable doubt, and

3. The accused cannot be detained without due process but must appear promptly before a Court, according to the principle of Habeas Corpus (Latin for "produce the body").

Both sides in a dispute are given equal time to file their statements and evidence, make motions to the Court, and respond to arguments. But to avoid "vexatious litigation" designed to simply harass or disrupt an adversary – which can drag out and impede justice and due process itself – the Court normally sets a strict time limit on pre-trial proceedings, after which the trial must commence.

The **pre-trial period** is designed to allow both sides the opportunity to present their evidence and arguments to one another in order to seek a settlement prior to a Court appearance. This presentation is usually referred to as **"Examination for Discovery"** or Voir Dire (**"to see and to say"**), where either party can demand any relevant evidence or document from the other.

If **Examination** does not produce a settlement of differences, then the Court is convened and a trial begins.

The general procedures and protocols of a Common Law Court are summarized in the following outline, which must be followed by anyone seeking to accuse and try other parties.

Step One – Compiling the Case

A **Statement of Claim** must be produced by those bringing a case, known as the Plaintiffs. Their Statement sets out in point form the basic facts of the dispute, the wrong being alleged, and the relief or remedy being sought.

Next, the **Plaintiff's Statement of Claim** must be accompanied by supporting evidence: documents and testimonies proving their case beyond any reasonable doubt. This evidence must be duly sworn by those not party to the dispute in the form of **witnessed statements**; and it must consist of the original documents themselves, and not copies.

As well, anyone whose testimony is used in this body of evidence must be willing to come into Court to testify and affirm their own statement.

Step Two – Seeking the Remedy of a Common Law Court: Filing a Notice of Claim of Right

After gathering his case, a Plaintiff must then seek the aid of a **Common Law Court and its officers.** Such a Court can be brought into being by **publishing a Notice of Claim of Right** (see Appendix B, "Court Documents"), which is a public declaration calling for the assistance of the community in the asserting of the Plaintiff's right under Natural Justice to have his case heard through the Common Law, by way of a jury of his neighbors and peers.

Such a Notice can be published in local newspapers or simply notarized and posted in a prominent public location, like a town hall or library.

Step Three – Forming a Common Law Court

Within 24 hours of the issuing of such a Notice of Claim of Right, any twelve citizens of a community can constitute themselves as a Common Law Court and its jury, and must then appoint the following Court Officers from their ranks:

- a **Court Adjudicator**, to advise and oversee the Court

- a **Public or Citizen Prosecutor** to conduct the case; this person is normally the Plaintiff himself or someone he authorizes to advise but not represent him

- a **Defense Counsel** to advise but not represent the accused

- a **Court Sheriff**, either elected from the community or delegated from among **existing peace officers**

- **Bailiffs**, a **Court Registrar** and a **Court Reporter**

It is assumed that people with knowledge of the Common Law and legal procedure will act in these capacities. And, as mentioned, a Common Law Magistrate or Justice of the Peace may also initiate this formation of a Common Law Court.

Step Four – Swearing in and Convening the Jury and Court Officers: Oaths of Office

Upon the appointment of these Court Officers, the Adjudicator (a Justice of the Peace or a comparable Magistrate) will formally **convene the Court** by taking and administering the following **Oath of Common Law Court Office** to all of the Court officers:

I (name) will faithfully perform my duties as an officer of this Common Law Court according to the principles of Natural Justice and Due Process, acting at all times with integrity, honesty and lawfulness. I recognize that if I fail to consistently abide by this Oath I can and will be removed from my Office. I make this public Oath freely, without coercion or ulterior motive, and without any mental reservation.

After taking this oath, the Jury members, Court Counselors, Sheriffs, Bailiffs and Reporter will then convene and receive instructions from the Adjudicator concerning the case. The Adjudicator is not a presiding Judge or Magistrate but an **advisor to the Court**, and has no power to influence, direct or halt the actions or the decisions of the Jury or other Court officers, except in the case of a gross miscarriage of justice or negligence on the part of other Court officers. Thus, **the Court is self-regulating and dependent on the mutual respect and governance of all the Court officers and the Jury.**

Step Five – Pre-Trial Conference

The Adjudicator brings together both parties in a pre-trial conference in an attempt to settle the case prior to a trial. If a settlement is not achieved, both parties must then **engage in a mandatory Examination of Discovery,** in which the evidence and counter-evidence and statements of both sides will be presented. After a period of not more than one week, this pre-trial conference will conclude and the trial will commence.

Step Six – Issuing of Public Summonses

No person or agency may be lawfully summoned into Common Law Court without first receiving **a complete set of charges** being brought against them and a formal **Notice to Appear, or Writ of Public Summons**. Such a Summons outlines the exact time, date and address when and where the trial will commence.

The Public Summons is applied for by the Plaintiff through the Court Registrar. The Summons will be issued under the signature of the Court Adjudicator and delivered to the Defendant by the Court Sheriff within 24 hours of **its filing in the Court Registry by the Plaintiff**. The Sheriff must personally serve the Defendant, or post the Summons in a public place and record the posting if the Defendant avoids service.

The Defendant has seven days to appear in Court from the date of service.

Step Seven – The Trial Commences: Opening Arguments

After an introduction by the Adjudicator, the trial commences with opening arguments by first the Plaintiff or Prosecutor, and then the Defendant. The Adjudicator and both Counselors will then have the chance to question either parties for clarification, and to make motions to the Court if it is apparent that the proceedings can be expedited.

Note: Step Seven can still occur even if one side, usually the Defendant, is not present in Court and refuses to participate. Such a trial, being conducted "in absentia", remains a legitimate legal procedure once the Defendant is given every opportunity to appear and respond to the charges and evidence against him. An In absentia trial will commence with the Plaintiff presenting his opening argument followed by his central case. The **Court-appointed Defense Counsel** will then be given the chance to argue on behalf of the absent Defendant, if that is the wish of the latter.

It is often the case that a **non-response** or **non-appearance** by the Defendant can result in the Adjudicator **advising the Jury** to declare a verdict in favor of the Plaintiff, on the grounds that the Defendant has tacitly agreed with the case against himself by not disputing the evidence or charges, and by making no attempt to appear and defend his own good name in public.

Step Eight – The Main Proceedings

Assuming the proceedings are not being conducted in absentia and the Defendant is present, the main proceedings of the trial then commence with the Plaintiff's presentation of the details of his evidence and argument against the Defendant, who can then respond. The Plaintiff may be assisted by the Citizen Prosecutor.

After his presentation, the Plaintiff is then cross-examined by the Defendant or his advising Counsel.

Following cross-examination, the Defendant presents his case, with or without his advising Counselor, and in turn is cross-examined by the Plaintiff or the Citizen Prosecutor.

Step Nine – Closing Summaries and Arguments to the Jury and final advice by the Adjudicator

After the main proceedings, the Adjudicator has the chance to further question both parties in order to give final advice to the Jury. The Plaintiff and then the Defendant then have the right to give their closing summary and argument to the Court. The Adjudicator closes with any final comments to the Jury.

Step Ten – The Jury retires to deliberate

The Court is held in recess while the twelve citizen jury members retire to come to a unanimous verdict and a sentence, based on their appraisal of all the evidence. There is no time restriction on their deliberations, and **during that time, they are**

not allowed contact with anyone save the Court Bailiff who is their escort and guard. The Jury's verdict and the sentence must be consensual, non-coerced, and unanimous.

Step Eleven – The Jury issues its unanimous verdict and sentence

The Court reconvenes after the Jury has come to a verdict. If the jurors are not in complete unanimity concerning the verdict, the defendant is automatically declared to be innocent. The **Jury spokesman**, chosen from among them by a vote, announces the verdict to the Court, and based on that verdict, the final sentence is also declared by the Jury.

Step Twelve – The Court adjourns and the Sentence is enforced

Following the announcement of the Verdict and Sentence, the Adjudicator either frees the Defendant or affirms and authorizes the decision of the Jury in the name of the community and its Court, and instructs the Sheriff to enforce that sentence. The Adjudicator then dismisses the Jury and formally concludes the trial proceedings, and the Court is concluded. The entire record of the Court proceedings is a public document, accessible to anyone, and can in no way be withheld, altered or compromised by the Adjudicator or any other party.

A Note on Common Law Enforcement: It is understood that every able bodied citizen is obligated and empowered by Natural Law to assist the Court Sheriff and his Deputies in enforcing the sentence of the Court, including by ensuring the imprisonment of the guilty, the monitoring of his associates and the public seizure of the assets and property of the guilty and his agents, if such is the sentence of the Court. This **collective law enforcement** is required in the interest of public safety, especially when the guilty party is an entire institution or head officers of that body.

A Note on Appealing Common Law Court Decisions:

Under the doctrine of Natural Law, in which every man and woman is born with an inherent grasp of right and wrong and of justice, it is understood that a jury of twelve citizens, when given the complete evidence and facts of a case, will arrive at a just and proper verdict. **The truth of that verdict must stand and is not subject to re-evaluation or dispute except in the case of a gross dereliction of duty or non-consideration of evidence.** Therefore, the verdicts of Common Law Court juries are not subject to appeal or revision, since the truth is not mutable or reformable.

This solidity of a verdict is also required by the **Common Law doctrine and custom of Stare Decisis, meaning "the decision stands", whereby the precedent decisions of previous Court verdicts have binding authority**. Without Stare Decisis, the law is subject to the whims and political interference of rulers and despots.

In the words of Black's Law Dictionary,

The doctrine of stare decisis states that legal decisions are binding and shall not be reversed. "The decision stands." That is, once a court has entered its judgment upon an issue, it shall not reverse itself. **This is in fact the foundation of legality in the common law system** – and is one of the principal differences between common and civil law.

Verdicts, Enforcement and Convicting Rulers and Institutions

Every legal system operates according to its own worldview and essential purpose. In the case of Civil or statute law, the contending interests of individuals waging war with one another in a courtroom define the process and aims of the Court. This system serves whoever has the money or influence to present the most convincing case, usually before a single magistrate who is part of a self-governing and unaccountable judicial clique.

The law, under this elite-derived system, is a private weapon to wield against another person or group over commercial interests, not an avenue of justice for all or of the common good.

In the Common Law, contrarily, the Court is defined not by contending individual interests, but by the needs of the community as a whole, and by justice as defined by those who have suffered from the lack of it. A bedrock of collective morality shapes how the Common Law operates, according to a simple issue: Will this legal decision and precedent best serve the community as a whole, and those within it who are the most vulnerable or who have suffered or been victimized, or who may so be?

Men and women have a natural tendency to resolve their differences and mediate disputes among themselves, when non-coerced and left to themselves to apply their own natural sense of right and wrong. Despite this, the State has under threat of force violently conditioned people to automatically deny their own judgment and defer to external authorities whenever they are in dispute or they seek justice. Therefore, **a long "relearning of freedom" is needed for Common Law to become a functional part of human life once again.**

Fortunately, we have found that the very act of publicly declaring and establishing the supremacy of the People and their Common Law has sparked that process of relearning freedom in the hearts and minds of growing numbers of people. Sparked, but not secured. For the greatest impediment to the efficacy of Common Law courts lies in the fears and doubts that seize citizens when they are presented with the power to be the law, and not have the law be done to them.

We have been taught wrongly that "Taking the law into our own hands", is a violation of civil order and tantamount to "anarchy". Whereas, **for citizens to judge legal matters for themselves is the highest civic virtue and the cornerstone of true democracy,** according to the Athenian law maker Solon.

The latter even believed that citizens should be fined or reprimanded for shrinking from a public controversy or from their inborn capacity to be lawgivers.

At the heart of that **personal responsibility for the law** is the capacity of citizens to judge a lawsuit for themselves as sworn jurors, and impose a verdict and sentence in such a suit. **The jury system has always been the purest expression of the Common Law and its capacity to empower the people themselves to defend traditional liberties and ascertain the truth of a matter.**

To render a fair and reasonable verdict, anyone simply needs to know all the facts and the evidence, and consider it all soberly, without threats, influence or coercion. **The more people who gather to determine the truth of a matter, the more likely they will come to a just and truthful verdict.** It tends to be the case that individual bias or prejudice, which is always present and undeniable within a jury, becomes through the jury process counter-balanced and absorbed into a **broader collective truth** imposed by the natural reason and fairness among jury members.

Enforcement

The big and thorny issue, of course, is not whether men and women can come to a Court verdict, but rather, how their decision can be enforced, and effective in their community. This is especially an issue when the verdict is imposed against heads of church or state, or even entire institutions, as in the February 25, 2013 verdict of the International Common Law Court of Justice (ICLCJ) concerning Genocide in Canada. (www.itccs.org)

To use that case as an example, **the moral weight of the verdict was clearly the strongest weapon in the arsenal of the Court**, and created the conditions for the enforcement of the verdict against the thirty officials of church and state named in the indictment.

For one thing, the February 25 verdict – which sentenced all the defendants to public banishment, twenty five years in prison and the loss of all property and assets – directly helped depose not only Pope Benedict, Joseph Ratzinger, but the most powerful Catholic Cardinal in Rome: the Vatican Secretary of State Tarcisio Bertone, who also resigned while in office after the ICLCJ verdict was pronounced.

Ratzinger and Bertone know about international law, even if others don't. They understand that the verdict of the ICLCJ carries a recognized legitimacy under the Law of Nations and the public right to form **Tribunals of Conscience** when governments and courts refuse to address a matter. And the Vatican also knows that the ICLCJ verdict can be entered into other nation's courts and used for the issuing of arrest warrants against proven war criminals like church officers. And so the resignation of these ostensibly "untouchable" church leaders in the spring of 2013 is simple proof of the power of independent, common law court verdicts.

A court verdict, after all, is a binding order carrying with it the full force of the law, and whoever ignores or subverts such a verdict, and the Court's orders arising from it, is guilty of an indictable crime.

In the Appendix to this Manual, we have reprinted all of the Court documents related to that first ICLCJ case of Genocide in Canada. The Court Order and Arrest Warrant dated March 5, 2013, can be acted on by any sworn agent of the ICLCJ or whoever such an Agent appoints. Any citizen, in short, can assist in the arrest of Joseph Ratzinger, Tarcisio Bertone and the twenty eight other officials of church and state found guilty of Crimes against Humanity by the ICLCJ.

Such enforcement of the law by citizens themselves is generally recognized in most countries, under the precedent known generically as "the Right of Citizens' Arrest". In

Canada, for example, under a law known as the Citizens Arrest and Self-defence Act (2012), citizens can detain anyone who either commits a crime or is even suspected of having done so, or who poses a threat to their own or others' safety: like, for our purposes, a child raping priest. This power of Citizens Arrest has in fact been broadened under this new Canadian law, from what it was previously.

(see: http://laws-lois.justice.gc.ca/eng/annualstatutes/2012_9/FullText.html)

In theory, then, the enforcement of Common Law Court verdicts by any citizen is not only perfectly legitimate and lawful, but is guaranteed even under the laws of countries dominated by Civil, statute law. But power, as we know, is not only about laws and theory, but ultimately involves naked force: the capacity of one group to impose its will upon another.

Hugh Grotius, a sixteenth century pioneer of international law, said that legal principles acquired power only when backed by cannon fire. So besides its legal and moral weight, what "cannons" will back up and enforce the verdicts of our Common Law courts? Especially when the fire power of those we are sentencing and arresting is apparently so much greater than ours?

Another great pioneer, the Chinese general Sun Tzu, wrote millennia ago that in any conflict, **power is not ultimately what you have materially but rather psychologically; and the superior firepower of a much bigger enemy can always be negated with the right, unforeseen maneuvers.** (We've reprinted forty of Sun Tzu's most relevant teachings in Appendix C).

Those rulers indicted by the ICLCJ are men and women garbed by the illusory robes of their offices, and they are guarded by other men and women who, like the rulers themselves, are motivated primarily by fear. That fear is their greatest weakness, and can be easily exploited by even a small group of people, as anyone who has occupied a Roman Catholic church learns very quickly.

The fact that laws guard the rich and the powerful is not as important as the reality that **any functional law rests upon its moral and political legitimacy.** Once such legitimacy is weakened or gone, the laws and hard physical power of a state or church begin to crumble. **Once public confidence in a ruler wanes, internal divisions appear in the ruling hierarchy, and usually a "palace coup" occurs and the regime falls.** We are witnessing precisely such developments and such a collapse of legitimacy within the Roman Catholic church today, in the manner of events prior to the deposing of any dictatorship.

And so the short answer to the question, how do we enforce our verdicts in the face of the power of the enemy, is simply, we do as Sun Tzu teaches, and strike at the weakest, not the strongest, part of that enemy.

The weak point of any institution, especially a church, is its public image and its source of money. Threaten either, and the entire institution must respond to the smallest of enemies. We have proven that in practice. And the very fact of our smallness gives us a freedom and flexibility to strike at such big targets when and how we like: a power that is denied to big institutions.

A Common Law Court verdict like the one of February 25 is a wedge between the credibility of an institution like the Vatican and the rest of the world. Clearly, by striking at that credibility – a weak link in the church's chain – we are maneuvering around the obvious strong points of that opponent and hitting them where they have no defense: **the fact that as an organization, they officially protect and aid child rapists and human trafficking.** And it was precisely by doing such a strategic maneuver that on August 4, 2013, **the Vatican was declared a Transnational Criminal Organization under international law.** (www.itccs.org, August 3)

As such a criminal body, the Vatican can now be legally disestablished, its officers arrested, and its property and wealth seized, not simply under Common Law but according to the Law of Nations. (see The United Nations Convention against Transnational Organized Crime, November 2000, articles 5, 6 and 12: http://www.unodc.org/unodc/treaties/CTOC/#Fulltext

So while it isn't normally possible to immediately detain heads of states or corporations after a sentence is passed against them, such an arrest does follow naturally as their credibility and protection diminishes. Their overt power tends to crumble as the law and public condemnation works around their strong defenses and undermines them, like water flowing around a wall or a rock.

The point of any Common Law Court verdict, after all, is not to target or imprison mere individuals, but to stop any threat to the helpless and to the community: to arrest such threats so they do not reoccur, primarily by ending the institutional source of those threats. And our chief means to do so is the moral weight of our evidence and verdicts combined with the capacity of many people to enforce those verdicts.

Common Law Sheriffs and Peace Officers

That brings us to a key aspect of the Court: its police arm, without which it cannot function.

The tradition of Common Law sheriffs is an old one in the English speaking world: men or women appointed from the local community to detain those harming others, bring them into town or "shire" courts for judgement, and enforce that court's sentence. In the United States, that tradition is still alive and embodied in locally elected sheriffs who are granted considerable power within their communities.

The role of the Common Law Court Sheriff is fourfold: 1) to provide security for the Court, 2) to deliver Court Summonses and Orders to Appear, 3) to detain and physically deliver to Court those summoned who evade a Court Order, and finally, 4) to enforce the final sentence of the Court, including by jailing and monitoring the guilty.

The Sheriff does not perform these duties alone, but with deputies and other agents he appoints to assist him. Such a "posse" is another pejorative term that actually refers to **an important traditional custom of mobilizing all the able bodied men in a community to stop anyone who has committed a crime.** The word "posse" comes from a Latin term "pro toto posse suo" meaning "to do the utmost in one's power".

According to one writer,

All persons who were the victims of a crime in Anglo-Saxon England were expected to raise their "hue and cry" and apprehend the criminal; and upon hearing their cry, every able-bodied man in the community was expected to do the "utmost in his power" (pro toto posse suo) to chase and apprehend the accused as a "posse".

- 1215: The Year of Magna Carta by J. Danziger et al (2003)

The custom of electing community peace officers like sheriffs, in other words, arose from the belief that everyone in a community had the obligation to police and protect themselves and their children. The Court Sheriff is thereby the servant of the people, taken from among them, answerable to and recallable by them, and not an external force over them.

Part of the power of such a Sheriff is that he can deputize anyone to assist him, including other police officers and agents of the very institutions being named and tried in Common Law courts. This is an especially important action and tactic during this, the early stages of the development of our local Common Law courts, since it uses the very strength of the system we are opposing against itself.

32

To give an example, if a Common Law Court Summons or Arrest Warrant is to be delivered against a church or government official, the Court Sheriff will first deliver a copy of it to the local, existing police agency along with a Deputizing Notice placing those police under the jurisdiction of the Common Law. (See Court Documents, Appendix B). As such, the police are then obligated to assist the Sheriff and must take the same Oath of Common Law Office as the Sheriff.

If those issued such a Notice deny or dispute it or refuse to take the Oath, they are then ordered to stand down from their position and to not interfere with the Sheriff in his duties. If they agree with the Notice, either directly or through their silence or non-interference, such police agencies are tacitly abiding by the Common Law action, and the normal protection around criminals in high office is suddenly nullified.

Such a remarkable encounter is in effect an enormous tug of war between two contending legal systems: a battle of wills, played out in full public view as an enormous "teaching moment". Our aim is to create and encourage such a creative confrontation and moral conflict at every level of official society.

This is the bigger and crucial point of that particular confrontation between Court Sheriffs and Civil law policemen, which must always be visible and televised to the world as it occurs: that it is a chance for the people to learn directly that **those policemen and soldiers who provide the muscle for the system are not exempt from the authority of Common Law, and must ultimately make a choice concerning who and what they serve.** The moral and propaganda value of publicly posing such a question is inestimable.

On those occasions when this tactic has been tested in Canada and elsewhere, the results have always been the same: the police back off and do not interfere. Time and again, neither the RCMP nor the Vancouver police have interfered with protestors who peacefully occupied Catholic or Protestant churches responsible for the death of Indian children. On one occasion, a senior police sergeant even stated that if the church had committed such crimes and were served with a Court Order, he'd be duty bound to enforce such an Order and help arrest those responsible!

Again, quoting Sun Tzu, to defeat an enemy one must know them; and such knowledge can only be gained through constant contact. "Provoke them to learn their responses. Prick them to test their strength and weakness. Do not outfight them but outthink them."

Common Law peace officers return power to the people by making them their own police authorities. In so doing, they challenge the very basis of the status quo and its elite-based rule, by undermining those unaccountable "armed bodies of men" who constitute the final and ultimate power of the State.

The Common Law, in short, is a seed of fundamental social and political transformation, not simply a weapon of self-defence for the oppressed.

On Citizens' Arrests

The right and necessity of citizens to detain suspected or actual criminals has long been recognized under both civil and common law.

For example, as mentioned, under a recent law in Canada, The Citizens' Arrest and Self Defense Act (2012), the right of citizens to perform arrests and detain suspects on their own has been broadened to include not only people caught endangering the community or harming others, but anyone suspected of crimes, including known offenders.

Under the same common law custom of pro toto posse suo (see above) that empowers any group of adults to unite and stop those causing harm, the right of Citizens' Arrest is not restricted or negated by a higher authority because of the recognition that any man or woman has the competence and obligation to see and directly halt wrongdoing in their community.

The procedure for performing a Citizens' Arrest is as follows:

1. One must first either witness a crime, or recognize a suspected criminal or known offender, or even have a reasonable suspicion that such persons pose a danger to others. Such a suspicion must be based on probable cause and not simply a "feeling" or prejudice about someone.

2. One must then inform the suspect or offender that he or she is being placed under Citizens' Arrest under the right of Necessity to Defend, which obligates the arrester to detain the suspect or offender. The arrester must state who they are and why they are exercising the power of arrest by stating the cause of action.

3. The offender or suspect must then be detained and held for trial in a common law court, if they turn out to have committed a crime or pose a danger to others. The amount of force used in the arrest must be a reasonable response to the suspect's behavior.

Citizens can normally hand over those they have detained to an authorized Common Law peace officer or a Sheriff of the court. The arresters must be willing to appear in court and give sworn testimony concerning their actions.

The crucial importance of the power of Citizens' Arrest is that **it trains and empowers citizens to take responsibility for policing their communities and for the law itself.** It moves democracy from theory to action.

Broader Consequences of the Common Law Court: A World made New

"Our first real step towards independence from England was

the establishment of our own Republican courts, right under the nose of the Brits. We set up a different legal system of our traditional Brehon laws, even while under military occupation. And we had to defend that system in arms. So you can say that once we started living under our own laws, everything else had to follow, right up to becoming a new nation."

- Joe MacInnes, Republican veteran of the Irish Civil War (1974 interview)

"For what you call the Law is but a club of the rich over the lowest of men, sanctifying the conquest of the earth by a few and making their theft the way of things. But over and above these pitiful statutes of yours that enclose the common land and reduce us to poverty to make you fat stands the Law of Creation, which renders judgement on rich and poor alike, making them one. For freedom is the man who will thus turn the world upside down, therefore no wonder he has enemies."

- Gerrard Winstanley, The True Levellers' Standard, Surrey, England, 1649

For the people themselves to sit in judgment of historically "untouchable" rulers like popes and heads of state, and to render an enforceable verdict on their crimes, **is a revolutionary act.** And such a revolution has begun, with the February 25, 2013 verdict of the International Common Law Court of Justice.

We cannot shrink from or deny the profound consequences of taking such a necessary historic step. Rather, we must recognize that the new judicial system in our hands is in fact a doorway to a transformed world, in which the land and its wealth and society as a whole is reclaimed by all people, and brought into harmony with Natural Justice through a great social levelling.

Many traditions and prophecies foresee such a time as now as a judgment upon the corruption and injustice of the human world.

Biblically, such a moment was known as the Jubilee, when all human laws and divisions are abolished, and society, like nature during a fallow year, is allowed to rest from warfare, corruption and injustice.

In truth, we recognize this historic moment not only as a condemnation of what has been, but primarily as a transformation into what is coming to be: a reinventing of humanity according to the simple principle that no law or authority shall ever again cause anyone to rule, harm or dominate others.

The aim of Common Law is to re-establish direct relations of mutual aid among people by placing justice and the law within their reach again. And that devolution of power will simultaneously disestablish all hierarchical institutions of state, business and church which control and mediate human life as a power over people.

A process so profound and revolutionary can only be enacted from the grassroots, by many people who have relearned freedom and use it to take action in their own communities to govern themselves as their own judge, jury and police. On the basis of this good renewed soil, a great harvest will one day arise in the form of new and local Republics of Equals, in harmony with itself and all Creation. The Common Law is a catalyst and a means towards achieving this political and spiritual end.

For now, as we struggle to give birth to the Courts that are like a great plow breaking open the dead soil of the status quo, **we must never forget that much of what we have been taught will betray us, for we have been raised as slaves to think and operate under laws that serve the few.** Everything must be rethought and retried according to the two great Principles of Natural Law: All things are placed in common for the good of all; and therefore, the law shall cause harm to no-one.

Our principles are firm, but our methods and tactics are supple. We must audaciously try ever new ways to expose, indict and stop the criminal institutions and corporations that are killing our planet, our children and our sacred liberties. And together, we must learn from every mistake and defeat, and generalize the victories and wisdom we gain into clear precedent, throughout this long redemptive struggle that will span many lifetimes.

The conscience born into us is our lamp during this journey and our best instructor, as is our great heritage of Natural Law and Reason, passed down to us so that a free and independent humanity may never perish from the earth.

Armed with this truth, this knowledge and this sacred purpose, go forth and take action! You have a world to win back.

"The Law is the public conscience. And the Common Law is but common reason." — **Sir Edward Coke, 1622**

……………………

APPENDIX

A. Sources and Resources

Bouvier's Law Dictionary, by John Bouvier, (1856) Legal Maxims, by Broom and Bouvier, (1856) A Dictionary of Law, by William C. Anderson, (1893) Black's Law Dictionary, by Henry Campell Black, (3rd, 4th, 5th, and 6th Editions, 1933-1990) Maxims of Law, by Charles A. Weisman, (1990)

See also O. W. Holmes, The Common Law (1881; new ed., ed. by M. DeWolfe Howe, 1963, repr. 1968); T. F. Plucknett, Concise History of the Common Law (5th ed. 1956); H. Potter, Historical Introduction to English Law and Its Institutions (4th ed. 1958); A. R. Hogue, Origins of the Common Law (1966); R. C. van Caenegem, The Birth of the English Common Law (1973); J. H. Baker, The Legal Profession and the Common Law (1986); R. L. Abel and P. S. C. Lewis, ed., The Common Law World (1988).

Further publications of aspects of the International Common Law Court of Justice and its procedures and principles will be forthcoming, issued by the ICLCJ Legal Advisory Board.

B. Examples of Common Law Court Documents

1. Notice of Claim of Right – To be publicly issued in order to convene a local Common Law Court.

PUBLIC NOTICE OF CLAIM OF RIGHT

Issued by _____

on _____

in the community of _____.

I, _____, give public notice of my personal claim of right and of lawful excuse to convene and establish a common law court under my liberty as a flesh and blood man or woman; and I do hereby call upon the support of all competent men and women to assist me in this lawful right.

I further give public notice of my personal claim of right and of lawful excuse to convene and establish as part of such a court a jury of my peers, consisting of twelve men or women, to judge a matter affecting the well-being, rights and safety of myself and my community, that matter being the following:

(Description of issue, statement of claim and parties named)

I further give public notice that the said jury of my peers claims the jurisdictional competence to judge this matter and issue a sentence and verdict within the said common law court established to render such a judgement, based upon proven and irrefutable evidence presented within its court.

I hereby publicly call upon and request the support of my community to establish this common law court and its jury of twelve men or women, to be sworn to act in such a capacity for the duration of the court proceedings, according to Natural Law and the rules of evidence and due process.

I make this public claim of right freely, without coercion or ulterior motive, in the interest of justice and the public welfare.

_____
Claimant

_____
(witness)

_____
Date

2. Deputizing Notice issued by Court Sheriffs to other Peace Officers.

NOTICE AND WARRANT TO DEPUTIZE — ISSUED UNDER THE AUTHORITY OF THE SHERIFF'S OFFICE OF THE COMMON LAW COURT OF JUSTICE — AND THE JURISDICTION OF NATURAL LAW AND THE LAW OF NATIONS

To all Peace Officers and Law or Statute Enforcement Officials:

This Public Notice is issued to you as a lawful warrant by the Common Law Court of Justice, placing you under the jurisdiction of the Court and Natural Justice, and deputizing you as its officers.

Upon your taking the appended Oath of Common Law Court Office (below), you are empowered to act as the lawful agents and protectors of the Court and its proceedings, and to serve and enforce its writs, warrants, summonses and court orders on any and all persons and corporations named by the Court.

If you choose not to take this Oath of Office, you are compelled and ordered by the Court and by Natural Law to refrain from interfering with the actions of other Officers so deputized and empowered to act for the Court.

If you resist, disrupt or impede the actions of the Court or its Officers you can and will be charged with criminal assault and obstruction of justice.

Issued on _____ in the Community of

_____ by the following Legal Agent or Sworn Peace

Officer or Sheriff of the Common Law Court of Justice:

_____

(signed)

(court stamp)

Oath of Common Law Court Office

To be issued to any sworn agent of the Court or to all persons or law enforcement officers deputized by the Court or its Sheriffs

I, _____, being of sound mind and clear conscience, do hereby swear that I will faithfully and justly execute the office of an agent of the Common Law Court of Justice according to the best of my abilities.

I understand that if I fail in my duties or betray the trust and responsibilities of my office I will forfeit my right to this position and can be dismissed.

I take this solemn oath freely, without coercion, reservation or ulterior motive, according to my conscience as a free man or woman, and as a citizen under the authority and jurisdiction of the Common Law.

_____

signed

_____

date

(court stamp)

3. Documents in the first case of The International Common Law Court of Justice, Docket No. 022513-001, In the matter of The People v. Joseph Ratzinger, Elizabeth Windsor et al. (Genocide in Canada)

(See attached hard copy documents and at www.itccs.org)

C. Strategy and Tactics: Forty Key Lessons from Sun Tzu:

1. One skilled in battle summons others and is not summoned by them.

2. One skilled at moving an enemy Forms and the enemy must follow; Offers and the enemy must take.

3. Form the ground of battle before engaging an enemy, on terms favorable to you. Then shape the ground to deceive the enemy, with actions that fit the enemy's own mind and action. Thus you form victory before battle by standing on the ground of no defeat.

4. Victory is not achieved by the physical destruction of an enemy but by their demoralization, which is accomplished by maneuver. Do not repeat successful maneuvers with the same enemy or they will recover and adapt to your tactics.

5. War is only a means to a political end, not an end in itself.

6. Knowing the enemy and knowing yourself: in every battle, no danger. Not knowing the enemy and knowing yourself: one defeat for every victory. Not knowing the enemy and not knowing yourself: In every battle, certain defeat.

7. Defend and one is insufficient. Attack and one has a surplus.

8. The victorious army is first victorious and then does battle. The defeated army first does battle and after that seeks victory.

9. It is the nature of warfare that swiftness rules. Everything will be won with swift action at the right moment, or lost without it.

10. Only fight an enemy if a position is critical; only move if there is something to gain.

11. Do not respond to the ground your enemy has prepared for you, but instead, shape their ground. Then they have no alternative but to be led by you, as if it was their own idea. This is skill.

12. Hide the time of battle from an enemy, and make what he loves and defends your first objective. When near, manifest far; when able, manifest inability, so as to confuse him.

13. Let your plans be as dark as night, then strike like a thunderbolt with utter surprise. Prior to such a surprise attack, feign weakness and offer the enemy a truce, to lull his defenses. The unexpected attack always negates the superior strength of an enemy.

14. If I do not wish to do battle, I mark a line on the earth to defend it, and the enemy cannot do battle with me. I misdirect him.

15. Respond to aggression by creating space, so as to control the actions of the aggressor. Resist and you swell the attacker. Create room for the aggressor and he will dissipate.

16. When I am few and the enemy is many, I can use the few to strike the many because those whom I battle are restricted.

17. Use order to await chaos. Use stillness to await clamor. At the right moment, not acting is the most skillful action. This is ordering the heart-mind.

18. It is not necessary to exercise your strength. Instead, rest in your sufficiency.

19. Every sage commander acts from his own ground of strength, which is formed solely by the completeness of his being. He accepts his nature and remains himself, which brings the power to discern clearly. The clarity and the will of the commander forms the ground of his entire army; and clarity comes from an honest and a humble heart.

20. The commander must never issue ambiguous orders.

21. The victorious commander does not win victory by conquering an opponent but by creating the larger view that includes both sides. Outthink, do not outfight, your enemy.

22. Always carefully discern the enemy's purpose. True knowledge of the enemy comes from active contact. Provoke them to reveal themselves, assessing their nature and responses. Prick them and know their movements. Probe them and know their strength and deficiencies.

23. An enemy can be subdued without battle once you understand the relationships and combination of things that constitutes its power. This skill of understanding exceeds one hundred victories in battle.

24. Power is found not in solid things but in the constant flow of relationships, which are never still. The power of a squirrel to cross a river on a log lies neither in the squirrel nor the log, but in their momentary combination. That combination is its power.

25. To employ the skill of understanding an enemy's power, one must be formless, like water. The water moves from high to low; your army's movements are determined fluidly, according to the state of your enemy. Thus is your power not fixed, and it is without permanent form, to reflect and capture the power of your enemy.

26. Never reinforce error or a defeat, but let your understanding move fluidly with each new experience. There is never a final or

definitive outcome to the army that moves like water.

27. Being without permanent form and fluid in your movements and tactics, you compel your enemy to defend against you at every point. He is thereby dissipated and weakened, and kept ignorant of your purpose while forced to reveal his condition to you.

28. By this means of formlessness, you can form the strongest enemy to the ground you have chosen for it, on the terms of your victory. But without foreknowledge of the ground itself, none of this is possible.

29. Hostile ground heightens your focus. Cut off from home support, you take nourishment from the enemy. Such supply lines cannot be severed. Use the threat surrounding you to stay united and sustain your army.

30. Place your soldiers where they cannot leave. Facing death, they find their true strength and cannot be routed. When they cannot leave, they stand firm and fight.

31. Extreme situations cause your troops to respond from profound sources of inner power. Training and commands cannot accomplish this. Dire circumstances automatically evoke it, unsought yet attained. The right relationships unleash enormous power greater than the individual parts.

32. If an enemy occupies high ground, do not engage him; if he attacks from high ground, do not oppose him.

33. If a mightier enemy pauses though enjoying an advantage, they are tired. If divisions appear in their ranks, they are frightened. If their commander repeatedly speaks soothing reassurances to his army, he has lost his power. Many punishments indicate panic. Many bribes and rewards means the enemy is seeking retreat.

34. Bind your own army to you with deeds. Do not command them with words.

35. Engage an enemy with what they expect, so that what you allow them to see confirms their own projections. This settles them into predictable patterns of response, distracting them from your actions while you wait calmly for the extraordinary moment: that which they cannot anticipate or prepare for. Use the extraordinary to win victory.

36. Be in this manner invisible and unfathomable to your enemy. To be thus without form, first be so orthodox that nothing remains to give you away. Then be so extraordinary that no-one can predict your action or purpose.

37. Thus, in battle, use a direct attack to engage, and an indirect attack to win.

38. Ride the inadequacies of your enemy. Go by unpredicted ways. Attack where your enemy has not taken precautions and avoid where they have.

39. Do not confront the enemy in their strength, but at the points of their weakness. Seize something the enemy holds dear. Their strength is then rendered useless; they must stop to listen and respond. Likewise, whatever you love makes you vulnerable. Prepare yourself to relinquish it.

40. Being thus prepared and awaiting the unprepared is victory. Thus it is said, "Victory can be known. It cannot be made".

In summary:

– Know your enemy and know yourself

– Subdue the enemy without fighting

– Avoid what is strong. Attack what is weak.

These three great Principles are tied together like braided strands of hair.

…………………

There is but one law for all, namely that law which governs all law, the Law of our Creator, the law of humanity, justice and equity. That is the law of Nature and of Nations. – Edmund Burke, 1780

For hard copies of this Common Law Court Manual, write to itccscentral@gmail.com. Donations for these copies can be through the ITCCS paypal system at www.itccs.org.

— — —

What is The International Tribunal into Crimes of Church and State? (ITCCS)

The ITCCS was formed in May of 2010 at a closed meeting of survivors of church and state terror in Dublin, Ireland. The event was initiated by Nobel Prize Nominee Reverend Kevin Annett of Canada and members of Irish survivors' groups.

The foundational purpose of the ITCCS is to unite survivors of genocide and child torture across borders, and to mount a broad political, spiritual and legal movement to disestablish the Vatican and other churches and governments responsible for historic and ongoing crimes against children and humanity.

The original ITCCS federation was composed of groups from Ireland, England, the United States, Canada and Italy, including the Templemore Forgotten Victims (Antrim, Ireland), the Friends and Relatives of the Disappeared (Canada), and United Against Church Terror (USA). By September, 2013, ITCCS had spread to twenty six countries and over fifty affiliated groups. Its work is translated into thirteen languages. Its affiliates include the prestigious cult ritual and abuse survivors' organizations SMART of the United States, and Rete L'Abuso in Savona, Italy.

The ITCCS operates from an undisclosed central headquarters in Brussels, Belgium, and from regional offices in Vancouver, New York, Dublin, London and Paris. ITCCS officers and their legal and political advisers generally retain their anonymity for reasons of security and safety. However, the General Field Secretary for North America and Western Europe is Kevin Annett. Other officers include Rev. Joshua Lemmens, Steve Finney and Amy Smart of Canada, Dr. George Dufort of Belgium, Rev. Ciaran Ui Niall of Ireland, and Dr. Colia Clark of New York City.

In September, 2012, the ITCCS established a legal arm, The International Common Law Court of Justice (ICLCJ), composed of accredited jurists and lawyers from Belgium, England and the United States. in February, 2013, the ICLCJ successfully prosecuted and convicted former Pope Benedict, Joseph Ratzinger, for Crimes against Humanity in Canada, along with Elizabeth Windsor, Queen of England, Canadian Prime Minister Stephen Harper, and 27 other officials of church and state. (See the link to the court evidence in this case at http://itccs.org) Pope Benedict and senior Vatican Cardinal Tarcisio Bertone both resigned from their offices soon after being prosecuted in this ICLCJ indictment.

To contact the ITCCS Central Office, write to itccscentral@gmail.com

Field Secretary Rev. Kevin Annett may be contacted at hiddenfromhistory1@gmail.com

---

See the evidence of Genocide in Canada and other crimes against the innocent at www.hiddennolonger.com and at the websites of The International Tribunal into Crimes of Church and State at www.itccs.org

An International, multi-lingual ITCCS site can be found at: http://kevinannettinternational.blogspot.fr/

The complete Common Law Court proceedings of Genocide in Canada are found at:

https://www.youtube.com/watch?v=UvhfXAd08TE – Common Law Court Proceedings – Genocide in Canada (Part One) – 1 hr. 46 mins.

https://www.youtube.com/watch?v=OPKFk_L7y9g – Common Law Court Proceedings – Genocide in Canada (Part Two) – 1 hr. 47 mins.

https://www.youtube.com/watch?v=ormOllOi4Vc – Final Court Verdict and Sentencing – 8 mins. 30 secs.

https://www.youtube.com/watch?v=IylfBxm3sMg – Authorizations and Endorsements of ITCCS/Kevin Annett by indigenous eyewitnesses – 10 mins.

https://www.youtube.com/watch?v=CReISnQDbBE – Irene Favel, Eyewitness to the incineration of a newborn baby by a priest at Muscowegan Catholic Indian school, Saskatchewan, 1944

https://www.youtube.com/watch?v=RBUd3UXt6fI – Other key testimonies from our Court case against genocide in Canada

What is the International Common Law Court of Justice?

The International Common Law Court of Justice (ICLCJ) – Founded as a lawful Citizens' Tribunal of Conscience on September 15, 2012 in Brussels

Natural and Customary Law allows for the establishment of popular courts of justice when the existing legal and governmental authorities are subverting the law and justice, or aiding those who do. Common Law arose historically to uphold the liberties of the people against tyrants, whether religious or secular, and accordingly, has universal jurisdiction when convened as a jury court by more than twelve duly sworn men and women.

The International Common Law Court of Justice (ICLCJ) was established as the legal and judicial arm of the International Tribunal into Crimes of Church and state (ITCCS), with the help of legal experts, judges and survivors of church terror and imperial genocide in more than a dozen countries. (www.itccs.org)

The first case in the docket of the ICLCJ commenced on November 6, 2012 and addressed the deliberate genocide of indigenous children in Canada by the Vatican, the Crown of England and other parties. In its final verdict of February 25, 2013, the Court and its fifty eight sworn citizen jurors successfully indicted and prosecuted thirty defendants for perpetrating or concealing this genocide. These defendants included then-Pope Benedict, Joseph Ratzinger, former Cardinal Tarcisio Bertone, Elizabeth Windsor "Queen of England", and Canadian Prime Minister Stephen Harper.

After an exhaustive presentation of the evidence of crimes by church and state in Canada, and a refusal by the defendants to respond or refute the evidence, all of the defendants were found guilty of criminal conspiracy and Genocide, and were sentenced in absentia to 25 years in prison and the forfeit of all the wealth and property of their estates and institutions. Citizen arrest warrants were issued, and on August 4, 2013, the Vatican and Crown of England were declared to be transnational criminal bodies under international law, and were lawfully disestablished.

The complete evidence that indicted these defendants and their institutions, along with all of the court documents and warrants, are contained herein:

https://www.youtube.com/watch?v=UvhfXAd08TE – Common Law Court Proceedings – Genocide in Canada (Part One) – 1 hr. 46 mins.

https://www.youtube.com/watch?v=OPKFk_L7y9g – Common Law Court Proceedings – Genocide in Canada (Part Two) – 1 hr. 47 mins.

https://www.youtube.com/watch?v=ormOIlOi4Vc – Final Court Verdict and Sentencing – 8 mins. 30 secs.

https://www.youtube.com/watch?v=RBUd3UXt6fI – Other key testimonies from our Court case against genocide in Canada

The International Common Law Court of Justice is proceeding with other cases during 2014 and beyond.

To contact the Court write to: itccscentral@gmail.com , attn: Mr. George Dufort, LL.B.

Reverend Kevin Annett of Canada

Kevin Annett is a Nominee for the Nobel Peace Prize (2013). Messages for him can be left at 250-591-4573 (Canada) or 386-323-5774 (USA).

*"I gave **Kevin Annett** his Indian name, **Eagle Strong Voice**, in 2004 when I adopted him into our Anishinabe Nation. He carries that name proudly because he is doing the job he was sent to do, to tell his people of their wrongs. He speaks strongly and with truth. He speaks for our stolen and murdered children. I ask everyone to listen to him and welcome him."* — **Chief Louis Daniels – Whispers Wind Elder, Crane Clan, Anishinabe Nation, Winnipeg, Manitoba**

Printed in Great Britain
by Amazon